George Thomson Ignaz Pleyel

# A Select Collection of Original Scotish Airs for the Voice

To each of which are added Introductory & Concluding Symphonies &

Accompanyments for the Violin & Piano Forte, by Pleyel. With Select &

Characteristic Verses by the most admired Scotish Poet

George Thomson Ignaz Pleyel

**A Select Collection of Original Scotish Airs for the Voice**
*To each of which are added Introductory & Concluding Symphonies &*
*Accompanyments for the Violin & Piano Forte, by Pleyel. With Select &*
*Characteristic Verses by the most admired Scotish Poet*

ISBN/EAN: 9783744796651

Printed in Europe, USA, Canada, Australia, Japan

Cover: Foto ©Thomas Meinert / pixelio.de

More available books at **www.hansebooks.com**

# A SELECT COLLECTION

## OF

# ORIGINAL SCOTISH AIRS

### FOR THE VOICE.

To each of which are added

Introductory & Concluding Symphonies &

Accompanyments for the Violin & Piano Forte, by

# PLEYEL.

With Select & Characteristic Verses by the most admired Scotish

Poets adapted to each Air, many of them entirely new.

### ALSO

Suitable English Verses in addition to such of the Songs as are written in the

### Scotish dialect.
Price 8:1h

DUBLIN Published by HIME at his Musical circulating Library Nº 54 College Green, where may hnd by the same Author, 12 SONATA'S in which are Introduced for the Subject of the Adagio's and last movements select Scotish Airs, with an Accompanyment for a Violin. Price each SONATA 2 : 8h.
NB. Great variety of new Music and Single Songs.

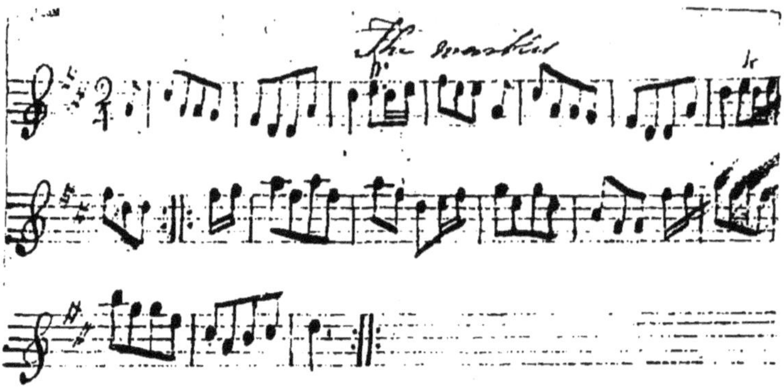

# CONTENTS

## OF THE

## FIRST SET.

# THE SMILING MORN

The smiling morn, the breathing spring, In-vite the tuneful birds to sing, and

while they war-ble from each spray, Love melts the u-ni-ver-sal lay. Let

us A-MAN-DA time-ly wise, like them improve the hour that flies, And

in soft raptures waste the day A-mong the birks of IN-VER-MAY.

# THE SMILING MORN, &c.

## BY MALLET.

---

AIR.—THE BIRKS OF INVERMAY.

The smiling morn, the breathing-spring,
Invite the tuneful birds to sing ;
And while they warble from each spray,
Love melts the universal lay :
Let us, Amanda, timely wise,
Like them improve the hour that flies,
And in soft raptures waste the day,
Among the birks of Invermay.

For soon the winter of the year,
And age, life's winter, will appear;
At this thy lively bloom will fade,
As that will strip the verdant shade :
Our taste of pleasure then is o'er,
The feather'd songsters please no more ;
And when they droop, and we decay,
Adieu the birks of Invermay.

---

## HERE *AWA, THERE AWA,* &c.

WRITTEN FOR THIS WORK,

BY ROBERT BURNS.

---

Here awa, there awa, wandering Willie,
Here awa, there awa, haud awa hame;
Come to my bosom, my ain only deary,
Tell me thou bring'st me, my Willie, the same.

Winter winds blew, loud and cauld, at our parting,
Fears for my Willie brought tears in my e'e;
Welcome, now Simmer, and welcome my Willie;
The Simmer to Nature, my Willie to me.

Rest, ye wild storms, in the cave of your slumbers,
How your dread howling a lover alarms!
Wauken, ye breezes! row gently, ye billows!
And waft my dear Laddie ance mair to my. arms.

But oh, if he's faithless, and minds na his Nanie,
Flow still between us, thou wide roaring main.
May I never see it, may I never trow it,
But, dying, believe that my Willie's my ain.

---

## ENGLISH *VERSES,* TO THE SAME AIR,

WRITTEN FOR THIS WORK,

BY PETER PINDAR, Esq.

---

Where is the smile that was heav'n to our eye?
Where is the voice that enchanted our ear?
Nought now around us is heard but the sigh;
Nought in the valley is seen but the tear?

Blest is the cottage thy charms shall adorn;
There will the moments be wing'd with delight;
Pleasure with thee shall arise at the morn;
Rapture retire with thy beauties at night.

Marian, thy form was a sun to our shade,
Chac'd were the glooms when it beam'd on onr plain,
Leave not, O leave not the verdures to fade;
Let not chill darkness surround us again.

Tell us what tempts thee to fly from our grove?
What is our crime that our valley should pine?
Say, dost thou pant for the conquests of love?
The hearts of our shepherds already are thine.

# HERE AWA THERE AWA.

Here a _wa, there a _wa, wand _er _ing WIL _ _ LIE Here a _wa, there a _wa, haud a _wa hame, Come to my bo _som my ain on _ly Dea _ _ rie, Tell me thou bring'st me my WILLIE the same.

# WHAT BEAUTIES DOES FLORA DISCLOSE

**DUET**
**Adagio**

What beauties does Flora disclose, How sweet are her smiles upon Tweed. yet MARY's still sweeter than

What beauties does Flora disclose, How sweet are her smiles upon Tweed. yet MARY's still sweeter than

those, both nature and fancy exceed.   No daisy nor sweet blushing rose, Nor all the gay

those, both nature and fancy exceed.   No daisy nor sweet blushing rose, Nor all the gay

flowers of the field, Nor Tweed gliding gently thro' those, Such beauty and pleasure does yield.

flowers of the field, Nor Tweed gliding gently thro' those, Such beauty and pleasure does yield.

# WHAT BEAUTIES DOES FLORA DISCLOSE?

BY Mr. CRAWFORD, (of the AUCHNAMES Family.)

AIR.—TWEEDSIDE.

WHAT beauties does Flora difclofe?
How fweet are her fmiles upon Tweed?
Yet Mary's ftill fweeter than thofe;
Both Nature and Fancy exceed.
No daify, nor fweet-blufhing rofe,
Not all the gay flowers of the field,
Nor Tweed gliding gently through thofe,
Such beauty and pleafure can yield.

The warblers are heard in each grove,
The linnet, the lark, and the thrufh,
The black-bird, and fweet-cooing dove,
With mufic inchant ev'ry bufh.
Come, let us go forth to the mead,
Let us fee how the primrofes fpring;
We'll lodge in fome village on Tweed,
And love while the feather'd folks fing.

How does my love pafs the long day?
Does Mary not tend a few fheep?
Do they never carelefsly ftray,
While happily fhe lies afleep?
Tweed's murmurs fhould lull her to reft,
Kind Nature indulging my blifs;
To relieve the foft pains of my breaft,
I'd fteal an ambrofial kifs.

'Tis fhe does the virgins excell,
No beauty with her can compare;
Love's graces around her do dwell,
She's faireft where thoufands are fair.
Say, charmer, where do thy flocks ftray?
Oh! tell me at noon where they feed:
Shall I feek them on fweet-winding Tay?
Or the pleafanter banks of the Tweed?

## BEHIND YON HILLS, &c.

### BY ROBERT BURNS.

AIR.—MY NANIE, O.

Behind yon hills where Lugar flows,
'Mang muirs, and mosses many, O,
The wint'ry fun the day has clos'd;
And I'll awa to Nanie. O.

Tho' weftlin winds blaw loud and fhill;
And it's baith mirk and rainy, O;
I'll get my plaid, and out I'll fteal,
And o'er the hill to Nanie, O.

My Nanie's charming, fweet and young;
Nae artfu' wiles to win ye, O:
May ill befa' the flattering tongue
That wad beguile my Nanie, O.

Her face is fair, her heart is true,
As fpotlefs as fhe's bonie, O;
The op'ning gowan, wat wi' dew,
Nae purer is than Nanie, O.

A country lad is my degree,
And few there be that ken me, O;
But what care I how few they be,
I'm welcome ay to Nanie, O.

My riches a's my penny fee,
And I maun guide it cannie, O;
But warld's gear ne'er troubles me,
My thoughts are a', my Nanie, O.

Our auld Guidman delights to view
His fheep and kye thrive bonie O;
But I'm as blythe that hauds his pleugh,
And has nae care but Nanie, O.

Come well, come woe, I care na by,
I'll tak what Heav'n will fend me, O:
Nae ither care in life have I,
But live, and love my Nanie, O.

---

## ENGLISH VERSES, TO THE SAME AIR,

### BY Dr. PERCY.

O Nancy, wilt thou go with me,
Nor figh to leave the flaunting town?
Can filent glens have charms for thee,
The lowly cot and ruffet gown?

No longer dreft in filken fheen,
No longer deck'd with jewels rare,
Say, canft thou quit each courtly fcene,
Where thou wert faireft of the fair.

O Nancy, when thou'rt far away,
Wilt thou not caft a wifh behind?
Say, canft thou face the parching ray,
Nor fhrink before the wintry wind?

O can that foft and gentle mien
Extremes of hardfhip learn to bear;
Nor, fad, regret each courtly fcene,
Where thou wert faireft of the fair?

O Nancy, canft thou love fo true,
Through perils keen with me to go?
Or when thy fwain mifhap fhall rue,
To fhare with him the pangs of wo?

Say, fhou'd difeafe, or pain befal,
Wilt thou affume the nurfe's care?
Nor, willful, thofe gay fcenes recal,
Where thou wert faireft of the fair?

And when at laft thy love fhall die,
Wilt thou receive his parting breath?
Wilt thou reprefs each ftruggling figh,
And cheer with fmiles the bed of death?

And wilt thou o'er his breathlefs clay
Strew flow'rs, and drop the tender tear?
Nor then regret thofe fcenes fo gay,
Where thou wert faireft of the fair?

Adagio
non troppo

Be _ hind yon hills, where Lu _ gar flows, mang muirs and mosses

ma_ny, O. The win_try sun the day has clos'd, and I'll a _ wa to NAN_NIE, O.

Tho' west_lin winds blaw loud and shrill; and its baith mirk and rai_ny, O. I'll

get my plaid, and out I'll steal, and o'er the hill to NAN_NIE, O.

# HEAR ME YE NYMPHS.

**Adagio**

Hear me ye Nymphs and ev'_ry_ Swain, I'll tell how PEGGY grieves me; Tho' thus I languish and complain A_ _las! she ne'er be_lieves me. My vows and sighs, like si_lent air, unheed_ed ne_ver move_ her, The bon_ny bush a_boon Traquair, 'twas there I first did love her.

## HEAR ME, YE NYMPHS, &c.

### BY Mr. CRAWFORD.

———

AIR.—THE BUSH ABOON TRAQUAIR.

Hear me, ye nymphs, and ev'ry swain,
 I'll tell you how Peggy grieves me;
Though thus I languish, thus complain,
 Alas! she ne'er believes me.
My vows and sighs, like silent air,
 Unheeded never move her.
At the bonny bush aboon Traquair,
 'Twas there I first did love her.

.....................

Yet now she scornful flies the plain,
 The fields we then frequented;
If e'er we meet, she shews disdain,
 She looks as ne'er acquainted.
The bonny bush bloom'd fair in May,
 Its sweets I'll ay remember;
But now her frowns make it decay,
 It fades as in December.

Ye rural powers, who hear my strains,
 Why thus should Peggy grieve me?
Oh! make her partner in my pains,
 Then let her smiles relieve me.
If not, my love will turn despair,
 My passion no more tender;
I'll leave the bush aboon Traquair,
 To lonely wilds I'll wander.

## ONE DAY I HEARD MARY SAY.

BY Mr. CRAWFORD.

━━━

### AIR.—I'LL NEVER LEAVE THEE.

One day I heard Mary say,
  How shall I leave thee?
Stay, dearest Adonis, stay,
  Why wilt thou grieve me?
Alas! my fond heart will break,
  If thou shou'dst leave me;
I'll live and die for thy sake,
  Yet never leave thee.

Say, lovely Adonis, say,
  Has Mary deceiv'd thee?
Did e'er her young heart betray
  New love that's griev'd thee?
My constant mind ne'er shall stray,
  Thou may'st believe me,
I'll love thee, lad, night and day,
  And never leave thee.

Adonis, my charming youth,
  What can relieve thee?
Can Mary thy anguish soothe!
  This breast shall receive thee.
My passion can ne'er decay,
  Never deceive thee:
Delight shall drive pain away,
  Pleasure revive thee.

But leave thee, leave thee, lad,
  How shall I leave thee?
O! that thought makes me sad,
  I'll never leave thee.
Where would my Adonis fly!
  Why does he grieve me?
Alas! my poor heart will die,
  If I should leave thee.

━━━━━━

# ONE DAY I HEARD MARY SAY.

One day I heard MARY say

How shall I leave thee. Stay, dearest A-DO-NIS, Stay Why will thou

grieve me A-las! my fond heart will break If thou shou'dst

leave me; I'll live and die for thy sake, Yet ne-ver leave thee.

# MY PATIE IS A LOVER GAY.

**DUET**
**Allegretto**

My PATIE is a Lo—ver gay, his mind is ne—ver mud—dy, his breath is sweet—er

My PATIE's a Lo—ver gay his mind's ne'er mud—dy his breath's sweeter

than new hay, his face is fair and rud—dy. His shape is hand—some middle size, he's stately in his

than new hay, his face is fair and rud—dy. his shape's handsome middle size he's stately

wawk—ing, The shi—ning of his een surprise, 'tis heav'n to hear him tawk—ing.

wawk—ing The shining of his een surprise, 'tis heav'n to hear him tawk—ing.

## MY PATIE IS A LOVER GAY.

### BY ALLAN RAMSAY.

---

AIR.—CORN RIGGS.

My Patie is a lover gay,
  His mind is never muddy,
His breath is fweeter than new hay,
  His face is fair and ruddy.

His fhape is handfome, middle fize;
  He's ftately in his wawking;
The fhining of his een furprize;
  'Tis heav'n to hear him tawking.

Laft night I met him on a bawk,
  Where yellow corn was growing,
There mony a kindly word he fpake,
  That fet my heart a-glowing.

He kifs'd, and vow'd he wad be mine,
  And loo'd me beft of ony;
That gars me like to fing finfyne,
  " O corn riggs are bonny."

---

## ENGLISH VERSES, TO THE SAME AIR.

---

Come, dear Amanda, quit the town,
  And to the rural hamlets fly;
Behold, the wint'ry ftorms are gone,
  A gentle radiance glads the fky.
The birds awake, the flow'rs appear,
  Earth fpreads a verdant couch for thee;
'Tis joy and mufic all we hear!
  'Tis love and beauty all we fee!

Come, let us mark the gradual fpring,
  How peep the buds, the bloffom blows,
Till Philomel begins to fing,
  And perfect May to fpread the rofe.
Let us fecure the fhort delight,
  And wifely crop the blooming day:
For foon, too foon it will be night.
  Arife, my love, and come away.

## WILL YE GO TO THE EWE-BUGHTS, MARION?

Will ye go to the ewe-bughts, Marion,
  And wear in the sheep wi' me?
The sun shines sweet, my Marion,
  But nae half sae sweet as thee.
    The sun, &c.

O Marion's a bonny lass,
  And the blyth blinks in her e'e;
And fain wad I marry Marion,
  Gin Marion wad marry me.
    And fain, &c.

I've nine milk-ewes, my Marion,
  A cow and a brawny quey;
I'll gi' them a' to my Marion
  Upon her bridal-day:
    I'll gi', &c.

And ye's get a green fey apron,
  And waistcoat o' London brown;
And wow but ye will be vap'ring;
  Whene'er ye gang to the town.
    And wow, &c.

I'm young and stout, my Marion;
  Nane dances like me on the green:
And gin ye forsake me, Marion,
  I'll e'en draw up wi' Jean.
    And gin, &c.

## ENGLISH VERSES, TO THE SAME AIR,

### WRITTEN FOR THIS WORK,

### BY PETER PINDAR, Esq.

O Marian, so sweet are thy kisses,
  Thou shouldst not thy shepherd refuse.
Behold! they are so many blisses,
  And nought, my dear girl, wilt thou lose.

Those lips were created for pleasure,
  Then, wherefore, deny thy poor swain?
Say, thou feelest the loss of the treasure,
  I'll give thee thy kisses again.

Then, Marian, most cheerfully deal 'em,
  By such presents thou can'st not be poor;
So fruitful thy lips when I steal 'em,
  They quickly are cluster'd with more.

# WILL YE GO TO THE EWE-BUGHTS MARION

Will ye go to the ewe-bughts MARION, and wear in the sheep wi' me? The

Sun shines sweet, my MARION, but nae half sae sweet as thee, The

Sun shines sweet my MARION, but nae half sae sweet as thee.

# MY SHEEP I NEGLECTED

Largo

My Sheep I neglected, I lost my sheep-hook, And all the gay haunts of my youth I for-

-sook, No more for A-MINTA fresh garlands I wove; for am-bition I said, would soon

cure me of love. O what had my youth with am-bition to do. why left I A-

-MINTA why broke I my vow. O give me my sheep and my sheep-hook re-store, and I'll

wander from love, and AMINTA no more.

# MY SHEEP I NEGLECTED, &c.

## BY SIR GILBERT ELLIOT.

AIR.—MY APRON DEARY.

My sheep I neglected, I lost my sheep-hook,
And all the gay haunts of my youth I forsook,
No more for Amynta fresh garlands I wove;
For ambition, I said, would soon cure me of love.
O what had my youth with ambition to do!
Why left I Amynta, why broke I my vow?
O give me my sheep, and my sheep-hook restore,
I'll wander from love, and Amynta no more.

Through regions remote in vain do I rove,
And bid the wide ocean secure me from love;
O fool! to imagine that ought can subdue,
A love so well founded, a passion so true.
O! what had my youth with ambition to do!
Why left I Amynta, why broke I my vow?
O give me my sheep, and my sheep-hook restore,
I'll wander from love and Amynta no more.

Alas! 'tis too late at thy fate to repine;
Poor shepherd, Amynta no more can be thine:
Thy tears are all fruitless, thy wishes are vain,
The moments neglected return not again.
O what had my youth, &c.

## FAREWEL TO LOCHABER, &c.

### BY ALLAN RAMSAY.

#### AIR.—LOCHABER.

Farewel to Lochaber, farewel to my Jean,
Where heartſome with thee I have mony day been;
For Lochaber no more, Lochaber no more,
We'll may-be return to Lochaber no more.
Theſe tears that I ſhed they are a' for my dear,
And not for the dangers attending on weir;
Tho' bore on rough ſeas to a far bloody ſhore,
May-be to return to Lochaber no more.

Tho' hurricanes riſe, and raiſe every wind,
They'll ne'er make a tempeſt like that in my mind;
Though loudeſt of thunder on louder waves roar,
That's naething like leaving my love on the ſhore.
To leave thee behind me, my heart is ſair pain'd;
But by eaſe that's inglorious no fame can be gain'd;
And beauty and love's the reward of the brave,
And I maun deſerve it before I can crave.

Then glory, my Jeany, maun plead my excuſe;
Since honour commands me, how can I refuſe?
Without it, I ne'er can have merit for thee,
And loſing thy favour I'd better not be.
I gae then, my laſs, to win honour and fame,
And if I ſhould chance to come glorіouſly hame,
I'll bring a heart to thee with love running o'er,
And then I'll leave thee and Lochaber no more.

## YE SHEPHERDS AND NYMPHS THAT ADORN, &c.

### BY WILLIAM HAMILTON, Esq. OF BANGOUR.

#### THE SAME AIR.

Ye ſhepherds and nymphs that adorn the gay plain,
Approach from your ſports, and attend to my ſtrain;
Amongſt all your number a lover ſo true,
Was ne'er ſo undone with ſuch bliſs in his view.
Was ever a nymph ſo hard-hearted as mine?
She knows me ſincere, and ſhe ſees how I pine:
She does not diſdain me, nor frown in her wrath;
But calmly and mildly reſigns me to death.

She calls me her friend, but her lover denies;
She ſmiles when I'm cheerful, but hears not my ſighs.
A boſom ſo flinty, ſo gentle an air,
Inſpires me with hope, and yet bids me deſpair.

I fall at her feet, and implore her with tears;
Her anſwer confounds, while her manner endears;
When ſoftly ſhe tells me to hope no relief,
My trembling lips bliſs her in ſpite of my grief.

By night while I ſlumber, ſtill haunted with care,
I ſtart up in anguiſh, and ſigh for the fair:
The fair ſleeps in peace; may ſhe ever do ſo!
And only when dreaming imagine my woe.
Then gaze at a diſtance, nor farther aſpire,
Nor think ſhe ſhou'd love whom ſhe cannot admire.
Huſh all thy complaining; and, dying her ſlave,
Commend her to heav'n, and thyſelf to the grave.

# FAREWEL TO LOCHABER.

Farewel to Lo_chaber, farewel to my JEAN, where heartsome with thee I have mo_ny days been, For Lochaber no more, Lochaber no more, we'll may _be re_turn to Lo_chaber no more. These tears that I shed they are a for my dear, And no for the dangers at _ tending on weir; Tho' bore on rough seas to a far bloo_dy shore, may _be to re_ turn to Lo_chaber no more.

# BRAW LADS ON YARROW BRAES

Andante

Braw Braw Lads on Yar-row Braes, Ye wan-der through the bloo-ming hea-ther; But Yar-row Braes nor Et-trick fhaws, can match the Lads of Gal-la wa-ter.

# BRAW LADS ON YARROW BRAES.

WRITTEN FOR THIS WORK,

BY ROBERT BURNS.

---

AIR.—GALLA WATER.

Braw, braw lads on Yarrow braes,
  Ye wander thro' the blooming heather;
But Yarrow braes, nor Ettrick fhaws,
  Can match the lads o' Galla water.

But there is ane, a fecret ane,
  Aboon them a' I loo him better;
And I'll be his, and he'll be mine,
  The bonnie lad o' Galla water.

Altho' his daddie was nae laird,
  And tho' I hae na meikle tocher,
Yet rich in kindeft, trueft love,
  We'll tent our flocks by Galla water.

It ne'er was wealth, it ne'er was wealth,
  That coft contentment, peace, or pleafure;
The bands and blifs o' mutual love,
  O that's the chiefeft warld's treafure!

---

# MARY'S CHARMS SUBDUED MY BREAST.

WRITTEN FOR THIS WORK,

By the Hon. ANDREW ERSKINE, of KELLIE.

---

THE SAME AIR.

Mary's charms fubdued my breaft,
  Her glowing youth, her manner winning,
My faithful vows I fondly prefs'd,
  And mark'd the fweet return beginning.

Fancy warmly on my mind.
  Yet paints that ev'ning's dear declining;
When raptur'd firft I found her kind,
  Her melting foul to love refigning.

Years of nuptial blifs have roll'd,
  And ftill I've found her more endearing;
Each wayward paffion fhe controul'd,
  Each anxious care, each forrow chearing.

Children now in ruddy bloom,
  With artlefs look attention courting;
Their infant fmiles difpel each gloom,
  Around our hut fo gaily fporting.

---

# BUSK YE, BUSK YE, &c.

## BY WILLIAM HAMILTON, Esq.

### AIR.—THE BRAES OF YARROW.

*A.* Busk ye, busk ye, my bonny bonny bride,
Busk ye, busk ye, my winsome marrow;
Busk ye, busk ye, my bonny bonny bride,
And think nae mair on the braes of Yarrow.
*B.* Where gat ye that bonny bonny bride?
Where gat ye that winsome marrow?
*A.* I gat her where I dare nae weil be seen,
Puing the birks on the braes of Yarrow.

Weep not, weep not, my bonny bonny bride,
Weep not, weep not, my winsome marrow,
Nor let thy heart lament so leave
Puing the birks on the braes of Yarrow.
*B.* Why does she weep, thy bonny bonny bride?
Why does she weep, thy winsome marrow?
And why dare ye nae mair weil be seen,
Puing the birks on the braes of Yarrow?

*A.* Lang maun she weep, lang maun she, maun she weep,
Lang maun she weep with dule and sorrow,
And lang maun I nae mair weil be seen
Puing the birks on the braes of Yarrow;
For she has tint hir luver luver dear,
Hir luver dear, the cause of sorrow,
And I hae slain the comeliest swain
That e'er pu'd birks on the braes of Yarrow.

Why runs thy stream, O Yarrow, Yarrow, red?
Why on thy braes heard the voice of sorrow?
And why yon melancholeous weeds,
Hang on the bonny birks of Yarrow?
What yonder floats on the rueful, rueful stream?
What yonder floats? O dule and sorrow!
'Tis he, the comely swain I slew
Upon the doleful braes of Yarrow.

Wash, O wash his wounds, his wounds in tears,
His wounds in tears, with dule and sorrow;
And wrap his limbs in mourning weids,
And lay him on the braes of Yarrow.
Then build, then build, ye sisters sisters sad,
Ye sisters sad, his tomb with sorrow,
And weep around in waeful wise
His haplefs fate on the braes of Yarrow.

Curse ye, curse ye, his ufelefs ufelefs shield,
My arm that wrought the deid of sorrow,
The fatal spear that pierced his breast,
His comely breast on the breast of Yarrow.
Did I not warn thee not to lue,
And warn from fight? But to my sorrow,
O'er rashly bald a stranger arm
Thou met'st, and fell on the braes of Yarrow.

Sweet smells the birk, green grows green grows the grass,
Yellow on Yarrow's banks the gowan,
Fair hangs the apple frae the rock,
Sweet the wave of Yarrow flowan.
Flows Yarrow sweet? as sweet as sweet flows Tweed,
As green its grass, its gowan yellow,
As sweet smells on its breast the birk,
The apple frae the rocks as mellow.

Fair was thy luve, fair fair indeed thy luve,
In flow'ry bands thou him didst fetter;
Tho' he was fair and well belov'd again,
Than me he never lued thee better.
Busk ye, then busk, my bonny bonny bride,
Busk ye, busk ye, my winsome marrow,
Busk ye, and lue me on the banks of Tweed,
And think nae mair on the braes of Yarrow.

*C.* How can I busk a bonny bonny bride?
How can I busk a winsome marrow?
How lue him on the banks of Tweed,
That slew my luve on the braes of Yarrow?
O Yarrow fields, may never never rain,
No dew thy tender blossoms cover;
For there was basely slain my luve,
My luve, as he had not been a luver.

The boy put on his robes, his robes of green,
His purple vest, 'twas my ain sewing;
Ah! wretched me! I little little kend
He was in these the fatal ruin.
The boy took out his milk-white milk-white steed,
Unheedful of my dule and sorrow;
But ere the tootid of the night,
He lay a corps on the braes of Yarrow.

Much I rejoic'd that waeful waeful day;
I sang, my voice the woods returning;
But lang ere night, the spear was flown
That slew my luve and left me mourning.
What can my barbarous barbarous father do,
But with his cruel rage pursue me?
My luver's blood is on thy spear,
How can'st thou, barbarous man, then woo me?

My happy sisters may be may be proud;
With cruel and ungentle scoffin,
May bid me seek on Yarrow brant
My luver nailed in his coffin.
My brother Douglas may upbraid,
And strive with threat'ning words to move me;
My luver's blood is on thy spear,
How can'st thou ever bid me luve thee?

Yes, yes, prepare the bed, the bed of luve;
With bridal sheets my body cover;
Unbar, ye bridal maids, the door,
Let in the expected husband luver.
But who the expected husband husband is?
His hands, methinks, are bath'd in slaughter;
Ah me! What ghastly spectre's you,
Come in his pale shroud, bleeding after?

Pale as he is, here lay him, lay him down,
O lay his cold head on my pillow;
Take aff, take aff these bridal weids,
And crown my careful head with willow.
Pale tho' thou art, yet brst, yet brst belov'd,
O could my warmth to life restore thee!
Yet lye all night between my breasts;
No youth lay ever there before thee.

Pale pale indeed, O lovely lovely youth,
Forgive, forgive fu fool a daughter!
And lye all night between my breasts;
No youth shall ever lye there after.
*A.* Return, return, O mournful mournful bride,
Return and dry thy ufelefs sorrow;
Thy luver heeds nought of thy sighs,
He lyes a corps on the braes of Yarrow.

---

# THY BRAES WERE BONNY, &c.

## BY THE REV. MR. LOGAN.

### THE SAME AIR.

Thy braes were bonny, O * Yarrow stream,
When first on them I met my luver,
Thy braes how dreary, O Yarrow stream,
When now thy waves his body cover!
For ever now, O Yarrow stream!
Thou art to me a stream of sorrow,
For never on thy banks shall I
Behold my luve, the flower of Yarrow.

He promis'd me a milk white steed,
To bear me to his father's bowers;
He promis'd me a little page,
To 'squire me to his father's tow'rs;
He promis'd me a wedding ring,—
Now he is wedd to his grave,
Alas! his watery grave in Yarrow.

Sweet were his words when last we met;
My passion I as freely told him!
Clasp'd in his arms, I little thought
That I should never more behold him!
Scarce was he gone, I saw his ghost;
It vanish'd with a shriek of sorrow;
Thrice did the water-wraith ascend,
And gave a doleful groan thro' Yarrow.

His mother from the window look'd,
With all the longing of a mother;
His little sister weeping walk'd
The green-wood path to meet her brother;
They fought him east, they fought him west,
They fought him all the forest thorough;
They only heard the clod of night,
They only heard the roar of Yarrow!

No longer from thy window look,
Thou hast no son, thou tender mother!
No longer walk, thou lovely maid,
Alas, thou hast no more a brother!
No longer seek him east or west,
And search no more the forest thorough;
For wandering in the night so dark,
He fell a lifeless corse in Yarrow.

The tear shall never leave my cheek,
No other youth shall be my marrow;
I'll seek thy body in the stream,
And then with thee I'll sleep in Yarrow.
The tear did never leave her cheek,
No other youth became her marrow;
She found his body in the stream,
And now with him she sleeps in Yarrow.

---

* The critical reader will observe, that in the first and third lines of the first verse, the interjection O is added, to suit the measure of the air;—but in general, that this kind are taken only when found absolutely necessary.
It is here to be observed, also, with respect to this as well as other Songs, that where the Air requires the first word of the line to be emphatic, and the Poet sometimes inadvertently throws this emphasis upon the second word or syllable,—the Singer has only in such a case to supply a quaver for the unemphatic first word.

# BUSK YE BUSK YE.

Affettuoso

Busk ye, busk ye, my bonny bonny bride, Busk ye, busk ye my win_some marrow

Busk ye, busk ye, my bonny bonny bride, and think nae mair on the braes of Yar_row.

Where got ye that bonny bonny bride, Where got ye that win_some mar_row?

I got her where I dare na well be seen, Pu_ing the birks on the braes of Yar_row.

# IN APRIL WHEN PRIMROSES.

**DUET**
**Andante**

*for*  *pia.*  *pia.*

In A-pril when Primroses paint the sweet plain, And summer ap- proaching re-

In A-pril when Primroses paint the sweet plain, And summer ap- proaching re-

-joiceth the swain; -joiceth the swain; The yel-low-hair'd Lad-die would of -tentimes

-joiceth the swain; -joiceth the swain; The yel-low-hair'd Lad-die would of -tentimes

go, To the wilds and deep glens, where the hawthorn trees grow. hawthorn trees grow.

go, To the wilds and deep glens, where the hawthorn trees grow. hawthorn trees grow.

## IN APRIL, WHEN PRIMROSES, &c.

### BY ALLAN RAMSAY.

———

AIR.—THE YELLOW HAIR'D LADDIE.

In April, when primrofes paint the fweet plain,
And fummer approaching rejoiceth the fwain;
The yellow-hair'd laddie would oftentimes go
To wilds and deep glens, where the hawthorn trees grow.

There, under the fhade of an old facred thorn,
With freedom he fung his loves ev'ning and morn;
He fung with fo foft and inchanting a found,
That Sylvans and Fairies unfeen danc'd around.

The fhepherd thus fung,—Tho' young Madie be fair,
Her beauty is dafh'd with a fcornful proud air;
But Sufie is handfome, and fweetly can fing,
Her breath's like the breezes perfum'd in the fpring.

That Madie, in all the gay bloom of her youth,
Like the moon is inconftant, and never fpoke truth,
But Sufie is faithful, good-humour'd, and free,
And fair as the goddefs who fprung from the fea.

That mamma's fine daughter with all her great dow'r,
Was aukwardly airy, and frequently four:
Then, fighing, he wifh'd, would parents agree,
The witty fweet Sufie his miftrefs fhould be.

———

## 'TWAS IN THAT SEASON OF THE YEAR.

### BY RICHARD HEWIT.

AIR.—ROSLIN CASTLE.

'Twas in that feafon of the year,
When all things gay and fweet appear,
That Colin, with the morning ray,
Arofe and fung his rural lay;
Of Nanny's charms the fhepherd fung,
The hills and dales with Nanny rung,
While Rofline caftle heard the fwain,
And echo'd back the chearful ftrain.

Awake, fweet mufe, the breathing fpring
With rapture warms, awake and fing;
Awake and join the vocal throng,
And hail the morning with a fong:
To Nanny raife the chearful lay,
O bid her hafte and come away;
In fweeteft fmiles herfelf adorn,
And add new graces to the morn.

O hark, my love, on ev'ry fpray
Each feather'd warbler tunes his lay;
'Tis beauty fires the ravifh'd throng,
And love infpires the melting fong:
Then let my ravifh'd notes arife,
For beauty darts from Nanny's eyes,
And love my rifing bofom warms,
And fills my foul with fweet alarms.

O come, my love, thy Colin's lay
With rapture calls, O come away;
Come while the mufe this wreath fhall twine,
Around that modeft brow of thine;
O hither hafte, and with thee bring
That beauty blooming like the fpring,
Thofe graces that divinely fhine,
And charm this ravifh'd heart of mine.

# 'TWAS IN THAT SEASON OF THE YEAR.

Andante

*pia.*

'Twas in that sea_son of the year, when all things gay and sweet ap_pear, That

CO_LIN, with the morn_ing ray, A_rose and sung his ru_ral lay.

Of NANNY's charms the shepherd sung, The hills and dales with NAN_NY rung, while

Ros_lin Cas_tle heard the swain, and e_cho'd back the chear_ful strain

# FROM THEE ELIZA I MUST GO.

**Larghetto**

From thee E _ LI _ ZA I must go, and from my native shore; The cru _ el fates be_

_tween us throw a boundlefs O _ cean's roar. But boundlefs O _ cean's roaring wide be_

_tween my love and me, They ne _ ver never can divide, My heart and foul from thee.

# FROM THEE, ELIZA, I MUST GO.

## BY ROBERT BURNS.

From thee, Eliza, I muſt go,
  And from my native ſhore:
The cruel fates between us throw
  A boundleſs ocean's roar:
But boundleſs oceans, roaring wide,
  Between my love and me,
They never never can divide
  My heart and ſoul from thee.

Farewel, farewel, Eliza dear,
  The maid that I adore!
A boding voice is in mine ear,
  We part to meet no more!
But the laſt throb that leaves my heart,
  While death ſtands victor by,
That throb, Eliza, is thy part,
  And thine, that lateſt ſigh!

## GIN LIVING WORTH, &c.

#### AIR.—THE WAEFU' HEART.

Gin living worth could win my heart,
  You wou'd na' fpeak in vain;
But in the darkfome grave it's laid,
  Never to rife again.
My waefu' heart lies low wi' his,
  Whofe heart was only mine:
And oh! what a heart was that to lofe;
  But 1 maun no repine.

Yet oh! gin heav'n in mercy foon
  Would grant the boon I crave,
And tak this life, now naething worth,
  Sin Jamie's in his grave.
And fee his gentle fpirit comes
  To fhew me on my way,
Surpris'd, nae doubt, I ftill am here
  Sair wond'ring at my ftay,

I come, I come, my Jamie dear,
  And oh! wi' what gude will
I follow, wherfoc'er ye lead,
  Ye canna lead to ill.
She faid, and foon a deadlie pale
  Her faded cheek poffeft,
Her waefu' heart forgot to beat
  Her forrows funk to reft.

## ENGLISH VERSES, TO THE SAME AIR,

O cease to mourn, unhappy youth!
  Or think this bofom hard:
My tears, alas! muft own your truth,
  And wifh it could reward.

Th' excefs of unabating woe,
  This tortur'd breaft endures,
Too well, alas! muft make me know
  The pain that dwells in your's.

Condemn'd like you to weep in vain,
  I feek the darkeft grove,
And fondly bear the fharpeft pain
  Of never-hoping love.

My wafted day, in endlefs fighs,
  No found of comfort hears;
And morn but breaks on Delia's eyes
  To wake her into tears.

If fleep fhould lend her friendly aid,
  In fancy I complain,
And hear fome fad, fome wretched maid,
  Or fee fome perjur'd fwain.

Then ceafe thy fuit, fond youth, O ceafe!
  Or blame the fates alone;
For how can I reftore your peace,
  Who quite have loft my own?

# GIN LIVING WORTH.

**Adagio**

Gin li_ving worth could win my heart, you

wou'd_na speak in vain _ _, But in the darksome grave it's laid, never, never to

rise a_gain. My wae_fu' heart lies low wi' his, whose heart was on_ly

mine _, And oh! what a heart was that to lose But I maun no re_pine.

# THERE'S AULD ROB MORRIS.

**DUET**
**Andante**

There's auld ROB MORRIS that wons in yon glen, he's the King o' gude

There's auld ROB MORRIS that wons in yon glen, he's the King o' gude

fel_lows and wale of auld men He has gowd in his cof_fers, he has

fel_lows and wale of auld men He has gowd in his cof_fers, he has

sheep, he has kine, And ae bon_ny Las_sie his dar_ling and mine.

sheep, he has kine, And ae bon_ny Las_sie his dar_ling and mine.

## THERE'S AULD ROB MORRIS, &c.

WRITTEN FOR THIS WORK,

BY ROBERT BURNS.

AIR.—AULD ROB MORRIS.

THERE's auld Rob Morris that wons in yon glen,
He's the king of gude fellows, and wale of auld men;
He has gowd in his coffers, he has sheep, he has kine,
And ae bonnie lassie, his darling and mine.

She's fresh as the morning, the fairest in May,
She's sweet as the ev'ning amang the new hay;
As blythe and as artless as the lambs on the lea,
And dear to my heart as the light to my e'e.

But oh, she's an heiress, auld Robin's a laird;
And my daddie has nought but a cot-house and yard:
A wooer like me maunna hope to come speed;
The wounds I must hide which will soon be my dead.

The day comes to me, but delight brings me nane;
The night comes to me, but my rest it is gane:
I wander my lane, like a night-troubled ghaist,
And I sigh as my heart it wad burst in my breast.

O had she but been of a lower degree,
I then might hae hop'd she wad smil'd upon me!
O, how past deferving had then been my bliss,
As now my diftraction no words can exprefs!

## THE NYMPH THAT UNDOES ME, &c.

THE SAME AIR.

THE nymph that undoes me is fair and unkind,
No less than a wonder by nature defign'd;
She's the grief of my heart, and the joy of my eye,
And the cause of a flame that never can die.

Her mouth, from whence wit obligingly flows,
Has the beautiful blush, and the smell of the rose:
Love and destiny both attend on her will;
She wounds with a look, with a frown she can kill.

The desperate lover can hope no redress,
Where beauty and rigour are both in excess;
In Sylvia they meet; so unhappy am I,
Who sees her must love her, who loves her must die.

## ONE MORNING VERY EARLY, &c.

SAID TO HAVE BEEN WRITTEN IN BEDLAM,

BY A NEGRO.

---

### AIR.—GRAMACHREE.

One morning very early, one morning in the spring,
I heard a maid in Bedlam who mournfully did sing;
Her chains she rattled on her hands, while sweetly thus sung she;
I love my Love, because I know my Love loves me.

O cruel were his parents, who sent my love to sea,
And cruel, cruel was the ship that bore my Love from me:
Yet I love his parents, since they're his, altho' they've ruin'd me;
And I love my Love, because I know my Love loves me.

O should it please the pitying pow'rs to call me to the sky,
I'd claim a guardian angel's charge around my love to fly;
To guard him from all dangers how happy should I be!
For I love my Love, because I know my Love loves me.

I'll make a strawy garland, I'll make it wond'rous fine;
With roses, lillies, daisies, I'll mix the eglantine;
And I'll present it to my Love when he returns from sea;
For I love my Love, because I know my Love loves me.

Oh, if I were a little bird, to build upon his breast!
Or if I were a nightingale, to sing my love to rest!
To gaze upon his lovely eyes, all my reward should be;
For I love my Love, because I know my Love loves me.

Oh, if I were an eagle, to soar into the sky!
I'd gaze around with piercing eyes where I my Love might spy;
But ah, unhappy maiden! that Love you ne'er shall see;
Yet I love my Love, because I know my Love loves me.

---

## HAD I A HEART FOR FALSEHOOD FRAM'D, &c.

### BY R. B. SHERIDAN, Esq.

---

### THE SAME AIR.

Had I a heart for falsehood fram'd, I ne'er could injure you;
For tho' your tongue no promise claim'd, your charms would make me true;
To you no foul shall bear deceit, no stranger offer wrong;
But friends in all the ag'd you'l meet, and lovers in the young.

But when they learn, that you have blest another with your heart,
They'll bid aspiring passion rest, and act a brother's part:
Then, lady, dread not their deceit, nor fear to suffer wrong;
For friends in all the ag'd you'll meet, and brothers in the young.

# ONE MORNING VERY EARLY.

One morning ve_ry ear_ly, one morning in the spring, I heard a maid in

Bed_lam, who mourn_ful_ly did sing, Her chains she rat_tled on her hands, while

sweetly thus sung she, I love my love because I know my Love loves me.

# O WALY WALY.

Affettuoso

O Wa_ly, Wa_ly, up the bank, and wa_ly, wa_ly down the brae, and wa_ly by yon burn_side, where I and my love wont to gae

I leant my back un_to an Aik, I thought it was a trusty tree, but first it bow'd and syne it brake, and sae did my true love to me

## O WALY WALY, &c.

AIR.—WALY WALY.

O waly waly up the bank,
　And waly waly down the brae,
And waly waly yon burn-fide,
　Where I and my love wont to gae.
I leant my back unto an aik,
　I thought it was a truftie tree;
But firft it bow'd, and fyne it brake,
　Sae my true love did lightly me.

O waly waly love is bonny,
　A little time while it is new;
But when it's auld, it waxeth cauld,
　And fades awa' like morning dew.
O wherefore fhou'd I bufk my head?
　O wherefore fhou'd I kame my hair?
For my true love has me forfook,
　And fays he'll never loe me mair.

Now Arthur-feat fall be my bed,
　The fheets fall ne'er be warm'd by me;
Saint Anton's wall fall be my drink,
　Since my true love's forfaken me.
O Mart'mas wind, when wilt thou blaw,
　And fhake the green leaves aff the tree?
O gentle death, when wilt thou come?
　For of my life I am wearie.

'Tis not the froft that freezes fell,
　Nor blawing fnaw's inclemencie;
'Tis not fic cauld that makes me cry,
　But my love's heart grown cauld to me.
Whan we came in by Glafgow town,
　We were a comely fight to fee;
My love was i' the black velvet,
　And I myfell in cramafie.

But had I wift before I kifst,
　That love had been fae ill to win,
I had lockt my heart in a cafe of gowd,
　And pin'd it wi' a filler pin.
Oh, oh! if my young babe were born,
　And fet upon the Nurfe's knee,
And I myfell were dead and gone,
　For a maid again I'll never be.

## HARD IS THE FATE OF HIM WHO LOVES.

### BY THOMSON.

THE SAME AIR.

Hard is the fate of him who loves,
　Yet dares not tell his trembling pain,
But to the fympathetic groves,
　But to the lonely lift'ning plain.

Oh, when fhe bleffes next your fhade,
　Oh, when her footfteps next are feen,
In flow'ry tracks along the mead,
　In frefher mazes o'er the green.

Ye gentle fpirits of the vale,
　To whom the tears of love are dear,
From dying lillies waft a gale,
　And figh my forrows in her ear.

O, tell her what fhe cannot blame,
　Tho' fear my tongue muft ever bind;
Oh, tell her that my virtuous flame
　Is as her fpotlefs foul refin'd.

Not her own guardian angel eyes
　With chafter tendernefs his care,
Nor purer her own wifhes rife,
　Not holier her own fighs in pray'r.

But if, at firft, her virgin fear
　Should ftart at love's fufpected name,
With that of friendfhip foothe her ear—
　True love and friendfhip are the fame.

═══════

AIR.—GILDEROY.

Ah! Chloris, could I now but fit,
    As unconcern'd as when
Your infant beauty could beget
    No happinefs nor pain.
When I this drawing did admire,
    And prais'd the coming day,
I little thought that rifing fire,
    Would take my reft away.

Your charms in harmlefs childhood lay
    As metals in a mine;
Age from no face takes more away,
    Than youth conceal'd in thine.
But as your charms infenfibly
    To their perfection preft;
So love as unperceiv'd did fly,
    And center'd in my breaft.

My paffion with your beauty grew,
    While Cupid, at my heart,
Still as his mother favour'd you,
    Threw a new flaming dart.
Each gloried in their wanton part;
    To make a beauty, fhe
Employ'd the utmoft of her art;
    To make a lover, he.

═══════════

**DUET**
**Andante**

Ah! CHLORIS cou'd I now but sit as un-concern'd as when your in-fant beau-ty

Ah! CHLORIS cou'd I now but sit as un-concern'd as when your infant beauty

could beget no hap-pinefs nor pain. When I this dawning did admire, And

could beget no hap-pinefs nor pain. When I this dawning did admire, And

prais'd the coming day, I lit-tle thought that ri-sing fire wou'd take my rest a-way.

prais'd the coming day, I little thought that ri-sing fire wou'd take my rest a-way.

# OH! OPEN THE DOOR.

Oh! o_pen the door, some pi_ty to shew, Oh! o_pen the door to me, —— Oh! Tho' thou hast been false, I'll e_ver prove true; Oh! o_pen the door to me, —— Oh!

# *OH, OPEN THE DOOR,* &c.

AS ALTERED

## BY ROBERT BURNS.

⸻

Oh, open the door, fome pity to fhew,
   Oh, open the door to me, Oh;
Tho' thou haft been falfe, I'll ever prove true,
   Oh, open the door to me, Oh.

Oh, cold is the blaft upon my pale cheek,
   But colder thy love for me, Oh:
The froft that freezes the life at my breaft,
   Is nought to my pains from thee, Oh.

The wan moon is fetting behind the white wave,
   And time is fetting with me, Oh;
Falfe friends, falfe love, farewel! for more,
   I'll ne'er trouble them, nor thee, Oh.

She has open'd the door, fhe has open'd it wide,
   She fees his pale corfe on the plain, Oh;
My true love! fhe cried,—and funk down by his fide,
   Never to rife again, Oh!

# WHEN WILD WAR'S DEADLY BLAST, &c.

WRITTEN FOR THIS WORK,
## BY ROBERT BURNS.

AIR.—THE MILL MILL O.

When wild War's deadly blast was blawn,
And gentle Peace returning,
And eyes again with pleasure beam'd
That had been blear'd with mourning;
I left the lines, and tented field,
Where lang I'd been a lodger,
My humble knapsack a' my wealth,
A poor and honest soldier.

A leal, light heart was in my breast,
My hand unstain'd wi' plunder;
And for fair Scotia, hame again,
I cheery on did wander.
I thought upon the banks o' Coil,
I thought upon my Nancy,
I thought upon the witching smile
That caught my youthful fancy:

At length I reach'd the bonny glen,
Where early life I sported;
I past the mill, and trysting thorn,
Where Nancy aft I courted:
Wha spied I but my ain dear maid,
Down by her mother's dwelling!
And turn'd me round to hide the flood
That in my een was swelling.

Wi' alter'd voice, quoth I, sweet lass,
Sweet as yon hawthorn's blossom,
O! happy, happy may he be,
That's dearest to thy bosom:
My purse is light, I've far to gang,
And fain wad be thy lodger;
I've serv'd my king and country lang,
Take pity on a soldier.

Sae wistfully she gaz'd on me,
And lovelier was than ever;
Quo' she, a soldier ance I lo'ed,
Forget him shall I never:
Our humble cot, and hamely fare,
Ye freely shall partake it,
That gallant badge, the dear cockade,
Ye're welcome for the sake o't.

She gaz'd—she redden'd like a rose—
Syne pale like ony lily,
She sank within my arms, and cried,
Art thou my ain dear Willie?—
By Him who made yon sun and sky!
By whom true love's regarded,
I am the man—and thus may still
True lovers be rewarded.

The wars are o'er, and I'm come hame,
And find thee still true-hearted;
Tho' poor in gear, we're rich in love,
And mair, we'se ne'er be parted.
Quo' she, my grandsire left me gowd,
A mailin plenish'd fairly;
And come, my faithful soldier lad,
Thou'rt welcome to it dearly!

For gold the merchant ploughs the main,
The farmer ploughs the manor;
But glory is the soldier's prize,
The soldier's wealth is honor;
The brave poor soldier ne'er despise,
Nor count him as a stranger,
Remember, he's his country's stay
In day and hour of danger.

## AT SETTING DAY, AND RISING MORN.
### BY ALLAN RAMSAY.

THE SAME AIR.

At setting day, and rising morn,
With soul that still shall love thee,
I'll ask of heav'n thy safe return,
With all that can improve thee,
I'll visit oft the birken bush,
Where first thou kindly told me
Sweet tales of love, and hid my blush,
Whilst round thou didst enfold me.

To all our haunts, I will repair,
By greenwood-shaw or fountain;
Or where the summer-day I'd share
With thee, upon yon mountain.
There will I tell the trees and flow'rs,
From thoughts unfeign'd and tender,
By vows you're mine,—by love is your's
A heart that cannot wander.

# WHEN WILD WAR'S DEADLY BLAST.

When wild wars deadly blast was blawn, and gen_tle peace re_turning, and eyes a_gain with pleasure beam'd, that had been blear'd with mourning. I left the lines and tented field, where lang I'd been a Lod_ger, My humble knapsack a' my wealth, A poor and ho_nest Sol_dier.

# THE NIGHT HER SILENT SABLE WORE.

**Adagio**

'S. The night her silent sable wore, and gloomy were the skies; of glitt'ring stars ap-pear'd no more than those in NELLY's eyes. When to her fa-ther's door I came, where I had of-ten been, I beg'd my fair, my love-ly dame, to rise and let me in.

# THE NIGHT HER SILENT SABLE WORE.

AIR.—SHE ROSE AND LOOT ME IN.

THE night her silent sable wore,
    And gloomy were the skies;
Of glitt'ring stars appear'd no more
    Than those in Nelly's eyes.
When to her father's door I came,
    Where I had often been,
I begg'd my fair, my lovely dame,
    To rise and let me in.

But she, with accents all divine,
    Did my fond suit reprove;
And while she chid my rash design,
    She but inflam'd my love.
Her beauty oft had pleas'd before,
    While her bright eyes did roll:
But virtue only had the pow'r
    To charm my very soul.

Then who would cruelly deceive,
    Or from such beauty part!
I lov'd her so, I could not leave
    The charmer of my heart.
My eager fondness I obey'd,
    Resolv'd she should be mine,
Till Hymen to my arm convey'd,
    My treasure so divine.

Now happy in my Nelly's love,
    Transporting is my joy;
No greater blessing can I prove;
    So bless'd a man am I.
For beauty may a while retain
    The conquer'd flutt'ring heart,
But virtue only is the chain
    Holds never to depart.

# THE HEAVY HOURS ARE ALMOST PAST.

## BY LORD LYTTLETON.

THE SAME AIR.

THE heavy hours are almost past,
    That part my love and me;
My longing eyes may hope at last
    Their only wish to see.
But how, my Delia, will you meet
    The man you've lost so long?
Will love in all your pulses beat,
    And tremble on your tongue?

Will you, in every look, declare
    Your heart is still the same?
And heal each idle anxious care
    Our fears in absence frame?

Thus Delia, thus I paint the scene
    When shortly we shall meet,
And try what yet remains between
    Of loit'ring time to cheat.

But if the dream that soothes my mind,
    Shall false and groundless prove;
If I am doom'd, at length, to find
    You have forgot to love;
All I of Venus ask is this,
    No more to let us join;
But grant me here the flatt'ring bliss,
    To die, and *think* you mine.

## SWEET ANNIE FRAE THE SEA-BEACH CAME.

AIR.—SWEET ANNIE.

Sweet Annie frae the fea-beach came,
　Where Jocky fpeel'd the veffel's fide ;
Ah ! wha can keep their heart at hame,
　When Jocky's toft aboon the tyde :
Far aff to diftant realms he gangs,
　Yet I'll be true as he has been ;
And when ilk lafs about him thrangs,
　He'll think on Annie, his faithful ain.

I met our wealthy laird yeftreen,
　Wi' gowd in hand he tempted me,
He prais'd my brow, my rolling een,
　And made a brag of what he'd gie :
What though my Jocky's far away
　Toft up and down the awfome main,
I'll keep my heart another day,
　Since Jocky may return again.

Nae mair falfe Jamie, fing nae mair,
　And fairly caft your pipe away;
My Jocky wad be troubled fair,
　To fee his friend his love betray;
For a' your fongs and verfe are vain,
　While Jocky's notes do faithful flow,
My heart to him, fhall true remain,
　I'll keep it for my conftant jo.

Blaw faft, ye gales, round Jocky's head,
　And gar your waves be calm and ftill :
His hameward fail with breezes fpeed,
　And dinna a' my pleafure fpill :
What though my Jocky's far away,
　Yet he will braw in filler fhine ;
I'll keep my heart anither day,
　Since Jocky may again be mine.

## TO FAIR FIDELE'S GRASSY TOMB.

### BY COLLINS.

THE SAME AIR.

To fair Fidele's graffy tomb,
　Soft maids and village-hinds fhall bring
Each op'ning fweet of earlieft bloom,
　And rifle all the breathing fpring.

No wailing ghoft fhall dare appear
　To vex with fhrieks this quiet grove ;
But fhepherd lads affemble here,
　And melting virgins own their love.

No wither'd witch fhall here be feen,
　No goblins lead their nightly crew ;
But female fays fhall haunt the green,
　And drefs thy grave with pearly dew.

The red-breaft oft at ev'ning hours,
　Shall kindly lend his little aid,
With hoary mofs and gather'd flow'rs,
　To deck the ground where thou art laid.

When howling winds and beating rain
　In tempefts fhake the fylvan cell ;
Or midft the chace upon the plain,
　The tender thought on thee fhall dwell.

Each lonely fcene fhall thee reftore,
　For thee the tear be duly fhed ;
Belov'd till life can charm no more,
　And mourn'd till pity's felf be dead.

# SWEET ANNIE FRAE THE SEA BEACH.

Sweet ANNIE frae the sea-beach came, where JOCKY speel'd the vessel's side; ah wha can keep their heart at hame, when JOCKY's tost a boon the tide! Far aff to distant realms he gangs, yet I'll be true as he has been, and when ilk lass about him throngs he'll think on ANNIE, his faithful ain.

# SHEPHERDS I HAVE LOST MY LOVE.

**DUET**
**Largo**

Shepherds I have lost my Love; Have you seen my AN __ NA? Pride of ev'ry sha_dy grove up_

Shepherds I have lost my Love; Have you seen my AN __ NA? Pride of ev'ry sha_dy grove up_

_on the banks of Ban _ na. I for her my home for_sook, near yon mis _ ty

_on the banks of Ban _ na. I for her my home for_sook, near yon mis _ ty

moun _ tain, Left my flock, my pipe, my crook Greenwood shade and foun _ tain.

moun _ tain, Left my flock, my pipe, my crook Greenwood shade and foun _ tain.

# SHEPHERDS, I HAVE LOST MY LOVE.

AIR.—THE BANKS OF BANNA.

Shepherds, I have loft my love;
 Have you feen my Anna?
Pride of ev'ry fhady grove,
 Upon the banks of Banna!

I for her my home forfook,
 Near yon mifty mountain;
Left my flock, my pipe, my crook,
 Greenwood fhade, and fountain.

Never fhall I fee them more
 Until her returning;
All the joys of life are o'er,
 From gladnefs chang'd to mourning.

Whither is my charmer flown?
 Shepherds, tell me whither?
Ah! woe for me, perhaps fhe's gone
 For ever and for ever.

www.ingramcontent.com/pod-product-compliance
Lightning Source LLC
Chambersburg PA
CBHW021640270326
41931CB00008B/1101